And
Another Thing . . .

ROBERT PAUL SMITH

W · W · NORTON & COMPANY · INC · *New York*

For my Mother

Contents

All Kinds Poems

Some Songs About My Sons

Some Long Poems

Tell Us a Story

Tell us a story, tell us a story, tell us a story!

All right, which story do you want?

Do you want the story of the young man who invents the
carburetor
And he meets this girl on a bus
And this girl has freckles on her nose
And he meets this other girl at the party given by the head
of the plant in which he works and she has gold lamé
on her back and is the boss' daughter
And the girl on the bus with the freckles on her nose is a
demon with a monkey wrench and looks even prettier
with smudges on the freckles on her nose
And the girl with the gold lamé wants him to pretty up
her apartment
And the girl with the freckles wants him to happy up her
life
And you can have a dandy illustration which has very
little to do with the story but looks very handsome
on the page?

No, not that story. We know that story. He marries the
girl with the freckles and sells the carburetor for a
large sum of money.

Oh, you know that story. Very well.

Do you want the story of the man who loves his wife
But oh you kid?

And his wife loves him, but he has forgotten all the little
things that mean so much to a woman and she is not
going to wait another day for flowers and kind words
and a little understanding of the role a woman plays,
what with baking powder and parent teacher associa-
tions and the memory of Rod who loved and left her
and is now coming back to Hilldale on a buying trip
and staying at the local hotel and the phone rings?

No, not that story. Rod is vulgar and twenty years is a
long time, and she wears the new hat home and her
husband says to her, "I love you, wife, oh you are
some kid."

Okay, let's get away from the slick paper. You want an
art-type story?

Goody, goody, an art-type story.

He is fifteen years old, and nobody understands him.
His father says, "Go soak your head, you."
His mother says, "Darling."
He has only one friend, an Armenian egg-dyer
Who lives over a pool-parlor.
The Armenian talks no English,
The boy talks no Armenian.

Tell Us a Story

They understand each other.
Leaving the Armenian one day
He passes the pool parlor
And see his father make the six ball in the side pocket.
Nobody talks Armenian any more, and the world is full of
　　a number of things, good and bad.

We seem to have heard that story before. We are tired of
　　that story.

Oh.
Would you care for an American-type story
With people named Rafe and Lafe and Tafe?
And hush-puppies and mush-puppies
Hoe cakes and corn rakes
If'n and ef'n
Eph and Lu-boy,
Shoats and houn's and knives and wives?
Fat back and flat back and
Rats and bottom land
And the village idiot?

Are they still a-writin' of the story? We heard the story,
　　seems if, seems like, 'pears to us, sho does, right
　　enough, yeah man.

I see.
You want the story about the boy and his dog?
The one about the bashful cowboy?

The one with the symbols?
The one with the words?
The one that converses on three levels at once?
The one in the bar, the one about the man who drinks too
    much and can never go to the Ludens' for dinner
    again?

Tell us a story, tell us a story, tell us a story.

Okay, but you won't like this one either.

Its about you.
You live in a desert.
You aren't very brave.
You aren't very bright.
You will live for a time
You will love for a time
You will blame other people
For what you do.
You will hate, you will lie
You will steal, you will cheat
And you will never never say that you do.

It's a very big desert and it's not going to get much nicer
Very quickly
Whatever you do about it.
If you want water in it, you had better start digging
All by yourself with your own two hands
And maybe you'll find water

Tell Us a Story

Or maybe you will just not
And then you will—

Tell us a story, tell us a story, stop the sermon and tell us a
story.

Okay.

Once upon a time, there was a . . .

Talking about It

A mosquito got into my little boy's bed,
Damn, blast, and damn again.
He's come out in a blister, a welt and a wen,
Damn, blast, and damn again.

The thermometer stands at ninety-two,
Damn, blast, and damn again.
It's going to get cooler, but heaven knows when,
Damn, blast, and damn again.

Damn it and blast it, thumbs down on the world,
The summer is dead but it won't lie down,
The sun's in the mist, humid and berled,
God's gone away from this perishing town.

My neighbor is painting his blistering house,
Damn, blast, and damn again.
Why must he be such a hard-working louse?
Damn, blast, and damn again.

My wife she is humid, and sweated and fretted,
Damn, blast, and damn again.
She needs to be coddled and patted and petted,
Damn, blast, and damn again.

In a tree is a bird who feels perfectly swell,
Damn, blast, and damn again.

Talking about It

With an un-liquid song that's a passport to hell
And that's where I'll send him as soon as I'm well,
Oh damn, oh blast, oh damn again.

* * * *

An icicle fell down the back of my neck,
Damn, blast, and damn again.
The wife is a quivering, shivering wreck,
Damn, blast, and damn again.

The thermometer stands at five below,
Damn, blast, and damn again.
We have oodles of ice and mountains of snow,
Damn, blast, and damn again.

Damn it and blast it, bad cess to the earth,
A tundra where cretins alone could find mirth,
A frigid and rigid and unfriendly sphere,
Did somebody say that the springtime was near?

Damn you and blast you, you ignorant clod,
You force me to doubt an omniscient God.
You're an oaf, you're a fool, you're a great clabberclaw
Don't you know that the springtime brings on the spring
    thaw?

Then my wife will storm and my son will howl,
And we'll hate the milkman deep in our bowel.
Oh you mug, oh you feeb, oh you ignorant crud
Have you lived in the country with suburban mud?

(17)

On the rug will be footprints so cozy and brown,
On the lawn we'll watch fledglings take off and drown,
And ringing the grass will be ranks, beds and rows
Of the non-blooming plants that the cold weather froze.

Springtime is screens, and summer you know,
And the fall is the time to prepare for the snow.
This is my personal cycle of seasons,
I watch myself lose my seasonal reasons.

A bat got into my top-story belfry,
Damn, blast, and damn again.
Live in the country, the country's helfry,
Wild laughter, hysterics and sobbing and then,
Damn, blast, and damn again.

Pockets

POCKET: A small bag or pouch; especially, a pouch attached to a garment, as for carrying money—*Funk and Wagnalls*

Hold on, Mr. Funk, stay, Mr. Wagnalls.

The heart has its reasons that philology
Knows not of.
For money?
Fie, Mr. Funk.
Woe, Mr. Wagnalls.
Open your book and let the life-stream in.

At eight, a small blue patch
On a pair of small blue overalls, in which to keep
In turn,
A finger, a spool,
Half of the cellophane from a cigarette package.
From which to let fall
A large iron spoon (for digging),
An acorn found in the place called the woods.
All these things perfectly replaceable.

At twelve, a large sack depending
Left side, right side,
Rear, rear,
From a pair of corduroy pants that whistle.
Containing, usually simultaneously,

(19)

A piece of chalk, four checkers studded with thumbtacks,
A piece of leather strap, most of a chocolate marshmallow
  bar
(Studded with lint)
A nickel, a dime, four pennies, a skate key, a Canadian
  dime,
A key, a piece of solder, a key,
The ruby from a dime-store ring
(Studded with street tar),
A single ball bearing, a Heinz pickle-pin with part of pin,
A jack-knife (purloined), the lens from a flashlight,
All these things being currency, they are taken together.
Also, small pieces of dirty paper, a portion of a shingle,
Horse-chestnuts or pig-nuts, according to the season,
And shamefully hidden, at the bottom of the pile
A clean handkerchief, containing removable braces
(Unstudded).

At fourteen, we begin to come close to
Mr. Funk and Mr. Wagnalls.
The pants are long, pockets the same in number,
Money makes its appearance, often reaching
Such heights as one dollar and twenty-three cents,
Including a street-car token from another city.
Cigarettes, in normal times,
With amber tips, with cork tips, with straw tips,
Being bought for such things and the novelty of the name.

Pockets

Preferred are Virginia, or Turkish, or Egyptian or Russian,
Particularly if possessing an unusual stink.
(Sometimes, of course, this is replaced by half an ancient
Plug of chewing tobacco, too dear for dispossessing,)
A pipe with an amber stem, or
Continuing in a direct line from the corduroy pants,
A whole chocolate marshmallow bar
(Studded with lint).
The dirty pieces of paper remain,
One being distinguishable as an outline for
A constitution of an eternal brotherhood.
There is a clean handkerchief, left pocket rear,
Comb complete with oily coating, right pocket rear,
And often
In the new pocket, inside jacket right,
A letter written in green or violet ink, backhand,
With little circles over the i's.
The wallet makes its appearance, left rear,
Containing primarily a small photograph,
Signed with purple or green ink.

From now on, Messrs. Funk and Wagnalls
Are defining with a will.
No novelty,
The sums of money increase,
The street-car token from another city disappears, and
Often finds its way into the pocket of a pair of

Brown corduroy pants that whistle.
The incidence of metal is higher,
Watches, clips, pencils, lighters, fobs, small never-sharp-
ened knives,
Containing for function only a nail-file.
More scraps of dirty paper, envelopes mostly,
Small cards with unknown names.

The decline is rapid, small rattling glass bottles,
Little rattling tin boxes,
A box of curious cigarettes (with something left out or
something put in).

A great deal later, we get to
A small pocket knife, very sharp
(Studded with bits of apple skin.)
And one very powerful pill.

From A to Z

A is for Atom
Surely small, perhaps round,
Which nobody's happy
That anyone's found.

B is for Breast
Of which ladies have two;
Once prized for their function,
Now for the view.

C is for the Common Cold
Curable?
No,
So,
Blow!

D is for Dream
Which allows us to sleep.
Entertaining, omnipresent,
Soporific, and cheap.

E is for Ego
Part of the psyche
Putter of thumb
In id's leaky dikie.

F is for Friendship
A quality which
Is native to children and puppies and sich,
Obsolete among women, obsolescent with men
And lacking in nations since Heaven knows when.

G is for God
How odd, he muses,
What man chooses.

H is for Heart
The organ divine
Sacred to lesions
And St. Valentine.

I is for I
To me a fact
To you a fiction
In any case, a useful diction.

J is for Jew,
Personage who
Confounds the many
By being so few.

K is for Kith and also for Kin
The familial result of original sin.

From A to Z

L is for Love
Of which have no doubt,
It's what everything else is all about.

M is for Man
Who does what he can
Not knowing, if any, the key
To, if any, the plan.

N is for No.
Brief way to say
Yea, maybe,
Occasionally nay.

O is for Optometry,
Science whose dream
Is the reconciliation of your personal mote
To the general public beam.

P is for Protocol
Procedure diplomatical
To ensure that very littical
Is done with great eclatical.

Q is for Quirk;
With you it's an idiosyncrasy
With him it's just like that jerk.

R is for Russia
A country where the common man
Lives in the same old misery
According to a brand new plan.

S is for Sanity
State rare and lonely,
Found in the first person singular only.

T is for Time
Whose nature is such,
There are only two amounts of it,
Too little or too much.

U is for Under
The Yonder
of Over.

V is for Venery
High spirits in you, low living in Henery.

W is for Where
To live.
For many,
Any.

X is for the spot
On which we dwell
Variously called
Earth, Heaven, Hell.

(26)

From A to Z

Y is for You
A projection of me
In which I seem to you to be not me, but he.

Z is for Zero
Numerical hero.
Hail, immortal button!
You *know* you're nuttin'.

Three Different People in the Same Bar

1.

They gimme uh trumpet.
When I was a kid, they gimme uh trumpet.
Chollie, they said, thassa trumpet, Chollie, you play it.
Stick this end inna ya mouth, Chollie, and blow hard.
Fool around, and stay away from those gahdamn pushcarts.
All-a-time pinchin stuff from those gahdamn pushcarts,
Ya gonna get uh knock in the head.

I kep it in uh papah bag unna thuh bed.
Once uh week I give uh quarter ta Joe De Angelis,
Guy inna pool pahlah, useta play inna band, he says.
I fool around. I learn to play uh little.
I don't read.
Joe De Angelis says he can read, but he don't teach me.
Except the six ball inna side pocket,
Clean azza whissle.

Frankie Jacobs he ast me to play once
And we make uh coupla bucks together.
He's onna pianna—yeah, the same Frankie Jacobs, yeah, the
    band-leader, yeah.
Foots Schafter onna bass, and some ginzo onna banjo.

Three Different People in the Same Bar

Yeah, banjo, you uh wise guy uh sumthin, all bands hadda
   banjo.

I get outa Manual Training, ya know what year it is?
1930 it is.
Great year fah music.
I put thuh horn back inna papah bag unna thuh bed.
Geez, did I scuffle.
Evah sleep inna subway with noospapuhs onya?
Great. Good fa tha character. Fine.

Evah play inna pit band inna burlesque?
Dames. Geez, what tired dames.
Guys inna front row. Geez. Sometimes you think—
Aaaaa.

They gimme uh trumpet, long time ago, when I was uh kid.
I'm uh artist now.
I play polly-rhythms.
Thass what they tell me.
I'm aheada my time.
Thass what they say.
Joey useta play trombone, now it's uh slush-pump.
Thass the story. Lickrish stick, they talk about,
Re-bop, who knows what else.
Ya know sumthin? I'm inna book by a Frenchman.
Yeah. I made uh revolution usin a cawfee container fa uh
   mute.

Ya know sumthin. I can't read yet.

Music, I mean.

I don't play very good, either.

Who knows?

2.

"She hadduh new look, uh 'ooh' look, a boy whatsamattuh
    witchoo look,

I gave her uh high sign, uh sly sign, uh boy how I wantchou
    fuh mine sign"

Waddia think? Ya think it's gottit? Ya think it's commer-
    shul, huh?

I think Guy might would go fah it. Ya think so?

                    Urrrrrrr.

Beg yah poddon. These gahdam pickles'll kill me, but I
    can't stop, ya know?

Ya know, I think thassa cute tune.

Boy girl kind. Thuh boy sings one line, thuh girl responds.

Like Ozzie and Harriet usetuhdo.

Hey, he does all right, huh, that Ozzie?

Smart, huh. Helluva Hooper they tell me.

Hey lissen, yah doin sumthin tanight?

We'll go over and let Larry see this, huh?

He'll sing it fah yuh, yeah?

                    Urrrrrrr.

Three Different People in the Same Bar

I wuz gonna be uh doctor, ever know that?
Some laugh, huh?
Nothin up here inna head.
Nothin.
Jist rocks.

3.

I remember the high school dance.
I sang.
I had a dress with organdie and rosebuds.
And matching shoes,
And my first brassiere.
I was the hottest thing since electricity.
The movies were the next stop. Me and Irene Dunne.
First band I was with, they put the boots to me.
Singing all night, and that bastard with the fuzzy overcoat
    every day.

In the bus.
Knocking at the door.
That crummy gin in those—
Aaaa. Hearts and Flowers. Curse of an Aching—
How corny can you get?

Can you get me a screen test?
Don't you want to give me an audition?
Hadn't I better stop by and see you later on? Room 419?

Don't you know a very big man who handles all the talent
at MGM?

I always cry.
When I get drunk.
Wanna know something very very funny?
This'll kill you.

Do you know that I am, I really am, the best singer in the
world?

Some Games

Millionairy

I want a cap with silver bells
I want a cat with long gray whiskers
I want fame at the middle of my life
And I could be happy with a million dollars.

I want a room with flowers in a bowl
I want a tree going "shhh" near my window
I want the sun to wear on my finger
And I would find useful a large sum of money.

"What will we do with this wistful dreamer?"
"Hell, give him the dough."

I want a book full of ready-made secrets
I want a picture that moves all the time
I want the moon to spread on a cracker
And a check in ten figures would cause me to smile.

"Shall we oblige this adorable creature?"
"Sure, give him the dough."

He put on his cap with the silver bells
Famous he walked, with the gray-whiskered cat,
Out of the room with the bowl full of flowers
Past the tree which kept going "shhh"
Wearing the ring of the sun on his finger

Reading the book with the ready-made secrets
Looking at the picture moving every minute
Eating the moon-spread delectable cracker
And having a perfectly wonderful time

Hearing behind him, like leaves in the autumn
Bills of large denominations
Falling on the ground.

De Gustibus and Non Disputandum, Hear!

Thirty-two canaries
Standing in a row
And every last one of them, singing like a bastard.
Do you think I like canaries?
Not me.

Twenty-nine bulldogs
Gathered in a circle
Each and every one of them, drooling like a madman.
Is it your idea I am fond of bulldogs?
You have someone else in mind.

Four and twenty apple trees
Standing in an orchard
Full of those goddam white blossoms.
You perceive I am fond of apple trees?
You are in error.

Sixteen cup custards
Smiling in their brown bowls.
Now you're talking, bud.
Slurp.

Tie Your Tongue, Sir?

One block away from my house is an office building.
On the office building there is a sign.
It says, "The Webbing and Edging Company."
They sell webbing and edging.

But I hear voices when I pass by:
"Good morning, Mr. Webbing, did you have a nice week-
   edge?"
"Thank you, Mr. Edging, it was nice, but on Sunday it
   turned a little web."

"You won't forget to come to my daughter's webbing, Mr.
   Edging?"
"Certainly not, I have her present all ready. I hope she likes
   dry-point edgings."

"How is Mrs. Edging?"
"The pain is webbing."

"How is Mrs. Webbing?"
"Well, you know how it is. She's not getting any younger.
   Frankly, she's edging."

"Goodnight, Mr. Webbing."
"Goodnight, Mr. Edging."

They sell the *best* wedging and ebbing.

(38)

Natural History Naturally

To him they were bitterflies
And little yellow bittercups.
On his lawn, the sour grass grew.

All around the lurch trees
And the quaking aspirin
All around the virus plants
The nevergreen grew.

In his trees the crones cawed,
In his pool the spike swam.
With nature all against him,
What's a man to do?

He ate wry bread,
Bitter butter,
Funny honey, and then
He heard the willow laughing
Saw the blooming things all blooming
As he sat there in the glooming
Hating women, hating men.

The Wagon Will Be Here Soon

Sometimes he wore a block zoot with knicker-knackers
His thews were gray swayed.
On his head a howler hat with a blue milk band
In his hand a mold-footed cane.

From time to time he grew a tooth-tache mush-brush
And parted his hair right down the riddle
Changed his shoes to thing-tipped rogues
And put on his head a bemberg.

His name was Spooner, his disposition disposable
His manner in-affable, his life ultra-retrospectable.

He died, of course, of a complication.

Lackaday

Today is not Sat or Sun or Mon or Tues
Or Wed or Thurs or Fri.
Today is Lackaday.
How did you sleep? Fair.
How do you feel? About the same.
What's new? Not much.
What do you know? Not a thing.
What'll you have? The usual.
What'll it be? The same all around.
Who did you see? The same old bunch.
What do you feel like doing? **Anything you say.**
Don't you think so? Sure do.
Wasn't he? Sure was.
Wasn't she? You bet.
Well . . . . Well . . . .
Today is Lackaday.

Fielding Error

Everything fell down.
The pillars fell on the pillows,
The clouds on the crowds.
The comets went plummeting
The plums went splattering,
The trees fell on the grass
And the grass on the ground
So that all was a litter:
Fountain pens and chocolate cake
Cement and girdles
Mountains of vacuum cleaners
And pools of Coca Cola.
The Empire State
And Angelo's pigeon-coop.
The pussycat fell on the dumpling.
Said God,
"Oops."

In the Beginning Was the Word

The world is out of joint, he said,
Dislocating his arm.
I cannot see the forest for the trees, he cried,
Hitting his forehead on a beech.
I was born too late, he said,
And the doctors marvelled at a twelve months' baby.
My heart is in my throat, he sobbed,
And choking, died.

Goodbye Hy and You Too, Hugh

Among my friends I
Number a man called Hy.

Included in the list, too,
Another man called Hugh.

Unless I get stronger
They will be my friends no longer.

Because I cannot go any further—
It is really conversational murther—
When I start out by saying, "Hello, Hy, how are you?"
Or "Hello, how are you, Hugh?

Obviously even a stronger-willed person than I
Cannot say, "Hi, Hy."
Could it be tolerated by you
To say, "What's new, Hugh?"

There would be the same strain
In Spain
With, "Que hay, Hy?"
The words would harass
In Paris
With "Comment allez-vous, Hugh?"

(44)

Goodbye Hy and You Too, Hugh

In the beginning of the conversation lies the end.
I will seek out a new friend.
If God is merciful
He will be named Perciful.

Frog

La grenouille
La rana
Die Frosch
Geesus
Crise
        Look
    At
  It
                Jump!

Time Upon a Once

Once there was a house with the ceiling on the floor.
Once there was a house with a window in the door,

And in the house there lived a dog who was a cat
Who wore a kind of coat that looked just like a hat.

The dog who was a cat chased a mouse who was a mink
And they kept all their money in the kitchen sink,

Which was quite all right, it never got wet,
For the faucet on the sink was a television set.

The television set was in fact a loaf of bread,
Which was really just as well, the mouse always said,

Because they didn't have an outlet in which to plug a plug
Electricity came running through the dining room rug.

They cut with a spoon, drank their tea with a knife
And lived a quite delicious and exciting life,

And if you called their house peculiar, they'd have told you
That a great deal depended on one's point of view.

Gesell, Spock, and Others
of that Ilg

"Father," say the children, as I brush them off my knee
"Daddums," speak the *kinder,* "give a little time to we."
"Fadder," say duh kiddies, "leave us talk together, three."
"All right," says old Popsy, "it is time for us to dwell
On the thing that crawls through window cracks,
The thing called a gesell.

"A gesell is crafty and slippy and thin;
Leave the window this far open, a gesell gets in.
Stuff paper, stuff cloth, put window-stripping in,
It won't do a single bit of good, a gesell gets in."

"Oooh," say the little ones, "Oooh," say the siblings,
"The gesell's the one that comes and does the midnight
    nibblings."
"Right," says old fadder, "but that ain't all,
Have you ever seen what slithers in the upstairs hall?

"It is the ilg, the ilg, the three-toed ilg
The amoeba-shaped, accordion-draped, leg-bowed ilg.
It rambles and it shambles and it looks like a puddle
But it's an ilg, ilg, ilg, and it leaves you in a muddle."

(48)

Gesell, Spock, and Others of that Ilg

"Oooh," say the wee ones, "Oooh," say the brothers
"Maybe fathers can't protect you, but what about
     mothers?"
"Dollings," says old Papa, "mothers have the private stock;
Didn't Mommy ever tell you about the night-noise spock?

"The spock is the one that goes crack in the night,
The spock is the one that's all sound and no sight
On the stairs when they creak, in the beds when they
     squeak
And the little ticky sounds that make you feel so weak—
That ain't no clock—that's a spock!"

"Go on, you old parent," say the children two,
"You're making this up and it just scares you.
Who'd believe in stuff like that
It's all so corny, so very old hat;
Who'd believe in stuff like *that?*"

"Just parents," I said, and let them have it
With a baseball bat.

Some Sad Songs

The Longest Poem in the World

I am going to write, someday, the longest poem in the
    world.
Intricate, wonderful, precise
Flowing as a river flows
Flying as a bird
Singing, singing, and so entirely true
It will melt the heart
And make us all love one another,
Sit in the sun,
Laugh, and watch the babies crawl through the soft grass
Making a happy noise.

It will be the longest poem in the world
And for days now I have been hearing it all at once
From beginning to end, all at once.
The words shining and flashing,
The furred words and the quiet mouselike words
The round words and the square words
Orange and green and pale yellow,
Sliding over each other
Kissing each other on the forehead
Rubbing under the hand like a puppy.

In my head a storehouse of words
And all of them nice.
All of them about love
And buttered rolls
And my girl.

It must be a nice world
For those who can, period.
Who can do it
Have it
Know it without asking why
Or how to hold it.

But I could never be it
Or do it
Or have it
I can only say it.

And I will keep on saying it
And, someday,
That will be the longest poem in the world.

Small Quiet Song

A long time ago in the big city
A young man rode in a subway car
And when he saw a beautiful girl
He walked over to her and said above the loud noise,
"Please let me talk to you and walk with you,
Because I am very lonely."
But that young man was not me.

One day in a city by the sea
A little boy saw a man with a bunch of balloons.
He spoke to his father, he spoke to his mother,
And they said yes, he might have a balloon,
If he would walk over and give the man the money.
The little boy walked over and gave the man the money,
And it was a beautiful balloon.
But that little boy was not me.

I was not the young man, I was not the little boy,
And I will not be the old man in the park
Who talks to his neighbor on the bench.

Twenty-Five Hours a Day

Do you remember the time when what you feared
Was death?
That was when you were a young man.
When the shape of fear was the vase of life
With not enough time to drink it.
Not enough minutes in the hour, hours in the day,
Days in the life.
That was fear when you were young.
Now you know that the real horror is
Seconds crawling, spilling over each minute's edge,
The hours crawling in a procession from horizon to
  horizon.
All the time in the world
But not enough life.

Self-Explanatory Poem

Bury my head, my head is dead,
Bury my head, says id.
Now then, cheerily, up we go
Up we go, says ego.

I want to be through, I want to be rid
I want to be *rid*, says id.
You may want all you want, but you can't make me go
You *can't* make me go, says ego.

I'll spit and I'll fume, I'll kick and I'll scream
I'll lie down on the floor and tantrum,

You will only wind up with a scar on your knee
Lots of dust in your hair and your antrim.

You can't boss me, says id with a roar

You can't kid me, kicking there on the floor
Look, here's a toy, here's a toy now
Get up and play with your lovely new poem
Get up, we're a great big boy now.

A Twist of the Rest

The children's eyes grow big, their mouths grow O's
They squirm in their chairs and squeal
As the god on the stage turns water into wine
Crepe paper into bridges, canaries into empty space.
The cards skitter in the air, the coins gleam and twist.
O, cry the children, and O, and the rabbit comes out of the
    hat.

But the god's throat is dry, his boiled shirt covers damp,
The pits of his arms trickle and his eyes are dry and fretted.
The rabbit is real. The hat is real. But he knows and the
    children do not
That the rabbit was in the hat all the time.
He knows
And the children do not
That what he counterfeits
Is what he cannot do.

Alone in the hall, the magician is the man who knows
That the only way to get a rabbit out of a hat
Is to put it in in the first place.

The children know that the only thing to believe
Is that there was no rabbit, that the man made the rabbit
That O, O, the man made a rabbit!

And Another Thing . . .

The tomato sat on the plate
And it looked like a tomato, like a real tomato
Not like a picture in a magazine.
It was red, mostly
But also it was yellow, somewhat
And, in places, orange
And, at the stem end, green.

The kitchen knife sat on the plate
And the tomato cut like a tomato
Resistant, to a degree
Soft, up to a point;
And some of the seeds stayed in
And some fell on the white plate.

The tomato tasted like a tomato,
And I said to the kids, who know tomatoes
As pure red, perfectly round, perfectly tasteless
Absolutely uniform wet globes that come in a cardboard
And cellophane package all year round
"Kids, time for you to taste a real tomato."

They did. And one of them looked at me
And said, "Is *that* what a tomato tastes like?"

Yes, my children, that is what a tomato tastes like.
But you can only get it in season.

(59)

So, at least, they have eaten a tomato.
But they will never eat Country Gentleman corn;
It does not grow very well,
It does not ship very well,
It does not look pretty, they tell me.
The rows are uneven and worms like it
And in all respects it does not compare with
That efficient, beautiful, good-shipping, good-packing
Worm- and blight- and rust-resistant, even-rowed and uni-
    form yellow hybrid.
Of course, the hybrid does not taste like corn
And the Country Gentleman does,
But you can only get it in season.

The poor little kids,
They will never know what blueberries taste like.
They've got a new thing now
Which you can get almost all year round.
It is round—rounder than any blueberry.
It is blue—bluer than any blueberry.
It is almost as big as a grape
And almost as wet as a plum
And in all respects it is a sensation
Except it doesn't taste like a blueberry.

Cream cheese comes in
A beautiful silver-paper package.
It is fresher than anything, read the label;

And Another Thing . . .

It is the one, the only, the original, read the label;
It lasts longer, spreads evener, and is so full of vitamins
You can hardly keep it in the package, read the label;
But there is something in it now called vegetable gum, read
    the label.
It makes it keep, it makes it spread, it is healthy as all get
    out, read the label.
But it tastes more like vegetable gum
Than cream cheese.

Sour cream doesn't pour any more.
It sits in the container, upside down
With the top off
And comes out in spoonfuls
And it's the richest, stiffest, most luxurious-looking sour
    cream
I ever saw.
It doesn't have any taste, of course,
But it certainly is creamy, you got to give it that.

And farmer cheese, which should be stiff enough
To stand in slices, because that's what makes it farmer
    cheese,
Comes in a pliofilm package which makes it stay wet and
    rich and soft—
Loud cheers—
And not farmer cheese at all.

Seckel pears, which anybody knows are sickle pears
Are supposed to be small and hard and lumpy and grainy
      as a piece of wood, as anybody knows.
This irritated somebody.
Now they are big and soft and smooth and wet
And taste like a Bartlett, only not as good.

Lord, what they have done with blackberries.
And those handy dandy strawberries, which come all year
      round
And taste nearly as good as blotting paper, but pretty,
Man, pretty!
And that wonderful white, vitaminized, homogenized milk
Which barely remembers it came from a cow.

I sit in my air-conditioned office
Listening to the radio telling what the men in the airplane
Found on the radar while they flew in their pressurized
Cabin, on instruments, through the nick-named hurricane,
And chew on a pencil.
I want to tell you, that's one thing that tastes right.
They're still making pencils with that old-time cedar flavor.
And you can get them all year round.

Dated Poem

I have lived in New York a long time now
And I have grown accustomed to many things.
But Lord, deliver me from Madison Avenue between 56th
    and 80th streets
And God, let me not ride on any more Madison Avenue
    buses.
Lexington Avenue buses are one thing,
They are full of characters, and drunks, and old ladies with
    bundles
And from 56th street on down, the driver thinks he is Flash
    Gordon.
Fifth Avenue buses jiggle and shake and pant and wheeze
And there is always an old lady with cherries on her hat
Who doesn't think people should smoke on the top deck
No matter what the signs say.
And there is usually a little boy who talks in a high clear
    voice
And the girl who has only a five-dollar bill
And the people who open and close windows.

All this I accept, and as I say, I have lived in New York a
    long time
And have grown accustomed to these things.
But Lord, please, no more rides on the Madison Avenue bus.

I do not mind the gay old dog with straw hat and blue and
     yellow band,
With the barber-pink on his cheeks,
The stiff butt, and the pin-striped flannel suit,
His soul sustained by the prospect of an afternoon
With old friends in a bar, drinking expensive whiskey,
Talking about that man in the White House,
And lying about a girl with a pink-and-white body.
Nor am I disturbed by the woman
Whose ankles do not fit in her shoes,
Whose hips do not fit in her dress,
Whose stockings are falling down, whose hat is awry,
Who carries a dozen notes written on the backs of en-
     velopes
And drops them in order,
And then drops her bag in picking them up,
Jamming her head in the belly of whatever brave soul
Is leaving by the rear door, as requested.
And it is no longer painful to watch the gawky young girl
Whose eyes search the car in fright,
Trying to find out who is looking at her, noting she is
     sixteen
And that she has blonde hair and black eyebrows.
And I will string along with the Western Union boy
Who has grown the mustache,
And the sharpie with the pinched-in waist
And trousers up to his armpit,

Dated Poem

And the women who talk about the blue dress and how it
    didn't fit.
Even the mama who has dressed her two little girls
In blue striped skirts and pinafores and straw hats
With flowers on them,
So that they look like an ad for Best and Company
In the Sunday Times.

But Good Lord, I cannot stand another
Bourgeois mama and bourgeois daughter
With their high voices pitched insistently
Against the riff-raff of the bus.
The mama who says, "Yes, Pierre's I think, it's as cheap as
    any,"
Mama's daughter who says, "They're going to Nantucket,
    of course, but they don't know when. They have to
    stay in town, naturally, to see Mr. Awful off to
    England."
Mama who says whatever she says in a voice that has
    nothing left
To identify her as a human being.
Daughter who is going to be mama
Just as soon as mama finds someone who doesn't mind
    braces on the teeth
A face like a rice pudding
A mind carefully constructed of small attitudes.
Now I know why the comrades hate the bourgeoisie

(65)

And no matter how wrong they may be about anything
    else,
Good Lord, you know they're right about that.
And the women most of all,
Sexless, mindless, hungerless, idea-less,
Any word at all ending with less.
And the bavarian cream begat
The rice pudding
And the rice pudding begat
The milk and crackers
And the milk and crackers begat
The arrowroot biscuit
And they were the lords of the earth.

I have lived a long time in New York
And I have grown accustomed to many **things**
But from the Madison Avenue bus,
Good Lord deliver me.

All Kinds Poems

The Water in the Lake

The water in the lake
Makes a smooth soft glove
For any hand.

The water in the lake
Makes a tight clear mask
For any face.

The water in the lake
Has a deep deep love
For all in the world
That's made of flesh.

Dream to be Taken on All Bad Occasions

I am sitting in a large room, with nothing to do until I
  want to.
It is (always) about ten o'clock in the morning of a spring
  day,
And through the window can be seen:
A small baby learning to walk—and not doing too well at it.
He falls again and again on, of course, light green grass,
Which hurts neither the grass nor his own wonderful
  bottom.
A tree which we will not define too closely—
Suffice it to say that it is at the same time in pale lime bud,
In full white flower, and hung with assorted noiseless
  finches,
Largely in shades of strawberry, light cigar-tan, and yel-
  low-finch yellow.
Add sun of a medium heat, a breeze to ripple the grass,
And one beautiful woman in sun-tanned skin, canvas shoes,
  and cotton dress.
Her hair is long and tied with a ribbon.
The walls of the house are white, and in the room I am in,
There are no pictures, but many windows and numberless
  bookshelves.

(70)

Dream to be Taken on All Bad Occasions

I have breakfasted on the Spanish oranges that I have never
    eaten,
A loaf of French bread baked by my own French baker in
    the kitchen,
And butter from the Jersey cow you cannot see or hear
    from the house.
The cow smells slowly and sweetly of clover.
The cream was yellow in a brown jug,
The coffee was black in a flowered cup big enough for two.
I wear no tie, no collar, no shoes.
I walk (always) over the red-brown polished floor in
    wonderful woolen socks which are the right length.
I have a new book, beautifully bound in colored paper,
I slit the pages with an enormously expensive knife
Bought for that purpose
And I have nothing to do until I want to.
In a little while the beautiful woman in the cotton dress
Will come into the room with a handful of field straw-
    berries
Staining her fingers a delicious scarlet.
She will sit on my lap,
With the baby in her arms.
We all laugh and we all eat the berries.
And we have nothing to do until we want to.

Mr. Mahler Is the Barber,
Mr. Buckley Is the Butcher

What has happened to the barber shop,
What has become of Sam Mahler the Square Deal Man?
The shop by the railroad tracks where I used to go
With my money in my hand
And hope there were a lot of customers
So I could see the naked ladies in the magazines?
I would have to say, "Mr. Mahler, mother says not to use
The clippers in the back."
Mother said, mother knew, father gave me the money
And Mr. Mahler would take the men first, a little boy has
   lots of time.

What has happened to Mr. Buckley the butcher,
The shop with the sawdust on the floor, the men with the
   high white aprons and the straw hats,
The soup bones, the chicken feet, the high wire stools with
   the wooden tops,
The lamb chops with the paper pants?
Roast beef on Sundays, the mashed potatoes, the gravy
   spoon
Coming down and making a hollow and turning, the gravy
   lake

Mr. Mahler Is Barber, Mr. Buckley Is Butcher

In the mashed potato mountain, forever and always, the
    gravy lake.
As sure as riced potatoes went with pot roast.
As certain as the platter piled with smelts in the Spring.
As regular as grape-jelly-making in the kitchen in August,
The women's faces boiling red, their sleeves rolled up, the
    jelly bag dripping, dripping.
This did not happen, this was not something that somebody
    decided.
This was so. This was.
Mr. Buckley was the butcher.
Mr. Mahler was the barber.
I lived at 282 Claremont Avenue, and I had a name.

Is there a dining-room table anywhere, any more, round
    and brown-black
And heavy, for doing homework on?
Does a Tiffany glass chandelier hang from any ceiling?
What has become of grape-arbors and rambler roses,
Of old men who passed out chocolate bars, peppermints,
Pears and pennies?
What has become of the curing of lumps on the forehead
By the firm application
Of the flat of a cold silver table-knife?

Why don't the girls wear middy blouses any more?
Any cuban heels?
Any tam-o-shanters?

Anyone for birch-bark canoes, for pillows saying
"I Pine For You And Balsam"?
Sweet-grass baskets?
Florida water?
Tangee lipsticks, orange and illicit?

How can the girls tell the summer secrets
If there is no ice-cream parlor with high wire seats,
Where is the man in the Moxie sign?
Where are the boys' high boots from the Army-Navy
With the pocket for the jackknife on the side?
Can you patch a bicycle tire with rubber bands any more,
Is the center of a golf ball still poison?
Is there some guy at some garage still telling lies about some
    Dixie at some laundry?
Who makes boomerangs, bird-houses, sewing-spool tanks,
Keeps rabbits, keeps pigeons, keeps polliwogs in a Mason
    jar?
Do kids still say, "Well, my father says . . . "
Does a kid still come to school and tell, with considerable
    pride,
About the licking he got?
Do you go to the principal's office any more,
Are there any inkwells to stuff full of blotting paper,
Is there a kid somewhere, somewhere, standing in a school
    yard,

Mr. Mahler Is Barber, Mr. Buckley Is Butcher

Clapping erasers?
Are you still tardy, not late, is there still a cloakroom,
Window poles, has anyone ever figured out whether you stand in
Assigned, assized, or sized place?

What has happened to the fathers sitting together on some-
    body's sun porch on a summer evening,
Where are the kids who used to play Red Rover under the
    lights on the summer streets,
Is there a man anywhere, any more, who says, "Well,
    politics, I don't know, I never talk politics, come on,
    let's play a little pinochle."
Where is the red-faced man with the creaking collar
Who wears silk shirts and striped flannels in the summer
And smokes cigars, says, "Have a real cigar, a twenty-five
    center,"
Adjusts his pearl stick pin, wears French lisle socks with
    clocks,
Sends down to the corner for a quart of peach ice-cream?

Are there little girls who wear wash-silk dresses, Roman-
    striped hair-ribbons, barrettes,
Is there any little boy holding his breath until he is ten,
    because his father has said he can have a Scout knife
    then
And not before?

Does anybody get a hundred dollars if he does not smoke
until he is twenty-one?
Do kids walk along a street and kick a can, just to kick a
can?
Do women really, really exchange recipes any more?

Not where I am.

In the barber shop they talk about the bomb.
The butchers don't wear straw hats any more.
The women talk about sibling rivalry.
The men smoke cigarettes with filter tips.
The kids watch television.
And nobody knows who anybody is any more.

Mr. Mahler is the barber.
Mr. Buckley is the butcher.
Please, please. Mr. Mahler *is* the barber!

Domestic Poem

The title says this is a domestic poem
And so it is
But that is not to say it will make my wife happy—
Not right away.

I was walking along the street today, thinking about people.
How they kill each other,
Starve each other,
Fear each other,
How they do all the things that people do.

I looked up to find myself on a street
Full of girls
Just out of offices and factories.

Offices where they filed things
And typed things
And took them down in shorthand.

Factories where they pricked things
And sewed things
And took five minutes to smoke a cigarette
In the can.

They came pouring out on the street
They were all beautiful.

The fat ones, the thin ones, the blondes.

The white ones and the black ones.

With their big breasts and their little breasts, their thin legs
and their fat legs.

Their firm little behinds and their big ripe butts,
That bounced and wiggled and snapped.

And I wanted each and every one of them.

They were all beautiful and all different
And for each a man who liked each one the way she was.

And that is why this is a domestic poem.

American Ladies Go Home

I get my check and I go to the store.
I buy a Volvex turntable
And a Prolapse pick-up
And a Turboid pre-amplifier
And a Shutshopf speaker
With the Seeboid woofer
And the Colvox tweeter.
I spend the next two days burning myself with a soldering
    iron,
Embedding little bits of wire in my fingers
And tracing wire A (the red one) from terminal V-1 to pin
    R2-x
Finally it is all done.
I turn on the most superb record player that ever has been.
My wife says, "It's too loud."

I get some birthday money and I go to the store.
I buy English gin—360 proof.
I buy French vermouth—280 proof.
I buy a thin glass pitcher.
I put in some gin
And a little vermouth
And a whole lot of ice
And I stir it gently

And top each glass with a piece of lemon rind
From which I have laboriously removed the quick,
And twisted once, gently.
It is clear as a bell and very cold
And far away the best Martini anyone has ever made.
My wife says, "It's too strong."

A rich uncle dies and leaves me a fortune and I go to the
store.
I buy a LaBanza-Mercurio
With underhead valves
A lipped-off camshaft
Fuel injection, fuel convection, fuel-subjection
Latex tires, mercury sparkplugs
An eighty-two-and-a-half axle and a diamond-point steer-
ing wheel,
Silk upholstery and cashmere top.
It is the jazziest car ever seen on land or sea, and we go for
a ride.
My wife says, "It's too fast."

I trade everything in and open a store for women,
Selling slow cars,
Weak gin,
And lo-fi record players.

It Takes a Heap

I have a little painter who's as sweet as he can be,
And he'll be glad to paper, and to plaster, and to spackle,
And all he wants from me is a great big fee
And a lien on my leg
And an eye
And a knee.

I know a little plumber, too, he couldn't be much more nice,
And he'll be glad to plumb, and to kitch, and to lav,
And all he asks of me is a great fat price
And first call on my kidney
And my liver
And my lights.

I have a little lawyer-man, who couldn't be any kinder,
And he'll be glad to search and negotiate and such,
And the only thing he wants is a king-sized binder
And divvies on my calf
And my left rear
Grinder.

I am a little mortgagor who has a great big mortgagee,
He'll bury me in dollar bills for any term of years,
And the only thing he wants in addition to his searching fee

Is a little firm priority
On half a dozen
Vertebrae.

But my soul, sir, my soul, homeless, pure, and lonely,
Belongs to the real-estate agent only.

Grand Piano

He thought for a long time and decided
That what he thought he needed
Was the biggest piano ever in the world.

It would be, say, as big as a house.
Each key would be as big, say, as a couch,
And there would be his friends on all the keys.
The dark friends on the white keys
And the light friends on the dark keys
And a red-headed girl with no clothes on, on f sharp.

If he rolled over to his right, and bounced, he'd play a lick
    in treble
And to his left, rolling slowly, a walking bass
And best of all, he could just lie still
And be the note that wasn't played
While his friends were making the music.

It would be like being inside the music
A place he'd always tried to get.

Jelly Roll in the morning
Gershwin in the afternoon
And all night long the blues.

He thought for a long time and decided
Nobody would ever build a piano like that
But all the same, he thought, it would be a hell of a piano.

Where Is the Apple with the Worm Inside?

Summer fruit's icumen in,
Lhude sing phew-phew;
Hybrided beyond belief
To a taste I never knew.

Raspberries as big as plums
Vegetable man to God is wotting.
He tells truth, but does not tell
Tasteth like the paper blotting.

Corn is early, corn is mellow
If you like white, you still get yellow
Row on row the kernels run, like unto a draughtsman's plan
Perfect they run, imperfect they taste—*where* is the coun-
    try Gentleman?

Dear God, send me a little white peach
Uneven, lumpy, full of fuzz,
Let me bite and find it tastes now
Like it used to was.

Let me have too a little plum
Partially brown, with a skin like paper

Let me bite and let my tongue
Slurp and curl and caper.

Dear fruit, be good
And let the stars be pretty.

Things That Own Me

A satinwood box with a lamb's-wool lining
Opening smoothly on a long brass hinge
And sitting there quietly, shining and gleaming,
A jointed fish of light green gold.

I see it.

A toast-colored cook-pot of clay without glaze
Inside, grain by separate grain, rice and saffron,
Shrimp and mussel, oil and garlic and sausage and peas.
Paella, paella that I eat with friends.

I taste it.

A boxwood flute with a windy timbre,
Holes that I cannot cunningly stop
But in my head the music that it breezes,
The songs that it whispers, the truth that it tells.

I hear it.

A piece of stone from another country's riverbed
Worn by the water to a loving shape
Clearer than Durer, than Modigliani more heartbreak
And dumb, dumb, speaking to the hands.

I feel it.

Hard dull soap in a scrap of straw paper
Telling my nose of moss in the woods,
Of apple-wood shavings in the hand-held plane
Of a yellow carnation, new pea in the pod.

I smell it.

Body, body, how nobler than the mind.

More about Girls

All beautiful things happen to me
When I am riding on a bus.
And yesterday, riding on the bus
I made a discovery—
Proud poet, unsilent on his peak in Fifth Avenue
The discovery; hush:
There are night-time girls
And day-time girls.
And it is startling to see a night-time girl
On the street, blinking and scurrying, in the sunlight.
Her hair is loose on her neck,
Folded still and moulded by the pillow.
Her lips are damp
And she is pale and dim
Melting on the street.
I don't remember ever meeting
A day-time girl
At night.

What Things Are Like

My mother used face-powder that smelled the way a
    Nabisco tastes.

There is a singer named Lee Wiley who sounds as butter
    spreads.

Eating the year's first Concord grapes is like suddenly being
    able to play the piano by ear.

And did you ever see the noise coming out of a tenor sax
    in the shape of a mouth?

Planing a piece of wood, having just honed the iron and set
    the frog to exact perfection and being right,

Curls of wood coming up like the dream of all renewal

Is the same as being able, by stretching your arms, to fly.

And salting a white radish, watching the grains heap in a
    snow

Is like the minute, the first time, you knew the girl wanted
    to kiss you too.

Hearing the Mozart quintet was like being able to cry after
    the child was born.

Seeing Modigliani was like knowing, and it being all right,
    that everybody would die.

Tasting the perfect lobster perfectly sautéed in the perfect
    sauce was a scroll in the air stating art would endure,

And morning light out of a long night rolling to you on
    the city side street

(90)

What Things Are Like

Was the waited drink of water that hurt your throat so
    wonderfully on the thirstiest of all days.
The killer pill that canceled out the broken wrist was like
    the minute the power came back in the dreadful
    winter.
The screaming of the starter that until then would not
    start in the lonely road,
The day the man said you could have the job,
The day in the hall you found you passed,
The day the fever thermometer found no fever,
The quarter in the lining of the empty pocket.

There were kisses.
The kiss that was a bed
A wound
An accomplishment
A handshake
A letter
A snake
A bribe
A payment
A sort of fruit
A kind of song
A way of saying something
A way of saying nothing.
Lying in bed with cool clean sheets is like drinking a glass
    of milk.

Getting the needed shot of whiskey is like a five-dollar bill
    in the hand.
Putting on a pair of woolen socks is like knowing your girl
    is loving.

I wonder what kind of face-powder my mother used.
I wonder what a Nabisco tastes like.

Dirty Old Lady

She stood on the city corner, in the summer's first noon
Turned, blind-eyed, to the sun.
Her arms crossed on her flat chest,
Her face, with the eyes' lids closed as marble,
Tipped to the sun.
Listening?
Drinking?
She took the sun.
Her feet were pitiful, clothed in grimed cloth
Her hair was chopped, and grey, and straight
And her face was beautiful
And still
And noble
As she stood, doing what she had to do
Drinking the sun
Doing what she willed to do
Stand in the sun
Alive in the world, while the crowd rushed by
To keep appointments
Eat tuna-fish sandwiches
Have manicures.
She saved the world that day.
Giving the sun something to shine on.

Some Songs about My Sons

First Song

I

When he was born, I did not see him.
When he was naked, I could not look.
The first day home, the red eyes
The blackened cord, the folded legs,
The terrible meager body, the poor little, sore little,
Cut little bud.
And all his smiles, they said, were gas.
And all the clutching of his fingers on my thumb, they said,
    were reflexes.

II

And then the day the fool nurse went, and he was ours.
We were scared, until we put him on the scale. I was then
    able to say
Eternity, I have the honor to inform you that my son out-
    balances
One Manhattan telephone book,
One apple-shaped paper-weight,
A brass jug filled with a variety of pencils
And a reputed Meissen plate of sentimental value.
He has since broken the plate,
To our tempered delight.

(97)

III

What does he do now, I mean, what does he do?
Does he talk, does he walk, what does he do?
He walks, sideways, holding on.
Sometimes he stands, holding on, waving his foot in the air.
He talks, he says 'bab' for 'bib,' he says 'Mom, mom,'
And he says 'daddy' when I am not there, he says 'diaper'
    when I am not there, he says everything but 'bab' and
    'mom' only when I am not there.
He laughs, he laughs a good deal.
He cries, especially between his breakfast
And our breakfast.
Eating his pablum at his breakfast,
Eating my rice krispies at mine.
He cries, always, before he falls asleep.
He laughs, always, to see the lather on my face.
Do, do, what does he do?
It's not so much what he does.
It's that he is.

IV

What shall we say to the small boy?
Shall we tell him the world is a fen,
Peopled with brutes,
Roofed with stupidity, anger and hate?
Shall we tell him that with us it is different,

First Song

That in the love we bear him, within the circle of our blood,
Only there is dignity, warmth, and time to smile?

We shall tell him neither of these lies.
We shall say only,
You are the biggest small boy that ever was
And you spin the humming top like nobody ever did.
Spin it, boy, spin it, you're a hell of a kid,
Spin the world like a top and we'll listen to it hum.

V

It took a long time.
There were many quiet corners.
A lot of talk.
Some misery.
Great fear.
Occasional happiness.
And then, the mind being eased, the body allowed function,
The chance taken, the hostage given, the peace risked,
The sun out, the clouds high, the earth grinding in a shout,
Behold the boy!
My girl, my wife, bloomed and her flesh is rich.
We stand erect in a room, greeting each other as equals.
Our pity and our love and our appalling weakness
Stands on his small feet, stamping with his straight legs
Saying syllables of much meaning and grave import.
Why, it was so simple.
Our love wanted to live.

No Kitten, He

My son, like a cat, lives in my house.
What a joke of cats and babies on women and men.
"Your house?" they say and mew,
"Your house? Come now, you live in my house,
And you are but an extension of my finger, my claw.
You are here because I need milk, because I need a thing **to**
    scratch,
A thing to sit on."

Until today, when my son stopped being a cat.
He stood at my knees, and crawled on my lap,
Not for my buttered roll, not for my eyeglasses,
Not to feed or to sleep,
But for love.

No more kitten in the house.
Puppy, now.

Boom Boom Boom

Walking down the street, walking down the street
With the sun in its shine, the dry in my throat
Autobus and carmobile trumpet in the traffic trees.

Walking down the street, walking down the street
With the air in its moist, the sleep in my eye
Gentlelady gentlemale rumble with their elbows out.

And divided I, cretin with the thinking soul
Genius with the chomping lust
Walk down the street, walk down the street
Damned and blessed, petted and pounded
Bearing thin book with stick-like slim poems
And new, blue, first potty chair
First potty chair
For my son,
Boom boom,
First potty chair for my son.

Song for Everybody

I am going to sing you a song, all full of muskrats, and
      guinea hens, and
Small brown dogs,
And lions and tigers and tulips.
Would you like me to put in a kangaroo?
A porcupine too?
Would you care for some violets and a Siamese cat,
And a goat with a collar?
I am going to sing you a wonderful song.
How about some food?
Some nice yellow butter, and a brown egg.
And a whole straw basket full of peaches?
Good.
Some cream, and a blackberry bush without brambles,

And a marble,
And a kite, and a red rubber ball.
This is going to be the best song ever,
And I'll put in everything you want.
Just give me time
And tell me what you want:
Perhaps a donkey,
And a collie,
And some roller skates,

Song for Everybody

        And a barn,
        And a stream,

        And—I almost forgot—
        As many polliwogs as you want;
        Frogs, newts, beetles, toads,
        A snake in a circle,
        Some grass in a clump.
        Hills, caves and a big round sun.
        Seven bears jumping through seven hoops,
        An elephant for you to show your belly to,
        A dog asleep on a round rag rug.
        Oh, I'll put in everything.
        I'll sing you a wonderful song,
        Just give me time.

Number One Boy Paints

My son painted a picture.
I have the picture, you can see.
My son painted a picture,
He painted it yellow and green and for me.

My boy took up a paintbrush
He painted a picture, it's here to be seen.
He painted a picture, a wonderful picture,
It's orange and yellow and green.

It's got nothing to do with art
It's all got to do with heart
He painted a picture, the reason he did it
Was so he could give it to me.

For months he would not paint a picture;
He'd rather just sit on a stool
And watch all the others who painted their pictures
Each Tuesday in nursery school.

Last Monday while driving him schoolwards
We were discussing the state of the world
Telephone poles, the centers of rolls
And the reason why lettuce is curled.

We also touched lightly on babies,
Pliers, Miss Myers and locks,

Number One Boy Paints

Shaving and shoes, climbing and glues
How differs a wolf from a fox.

I said to him, son, it is paint-day;
He continued to talk of a tree.
Then he said it was not, but tomorrow it is.
I said, son, paint a picture tomorrow for me.

He said he would certainly do it.
He did it, it's there, look and see.
My son painted a picture, a wonderful picture,
He painted it yellow and green and for me.

Number Two Boy Fights

My son is not yet three,
And this soon his father has betrayed him.
"Don't cry," I said, "what's there to cry about?"
And over the spilled sugar he was spooning out, his face
    crumples
And he makes his moan again.

If I were better, I would say
And keep on saying for all my life
"Cry! Cry and complain!"
Weep for the spilled sugar
The broken toy
The lost love
The insolence and the disregard.
The stone wall is not for the jumping, but for being a wall.
The closed door will not open: it a thing to know.
The proffered love is returned, the locked heart stays
    locked.

It is a thing to know, but not to believe and never to accept.

The sugar should not spill!
Or the love be lost
Or anything in the world your excellence deserves

Number Two Boy Fights

Be withheld, without knowing the loss.
Grieve, grieve, rant and rave!

Spit in their eye, kid!
Mine first.

The Bravest One

Sing hey sing hallelujah, this day a great victory has been
    won.
There are two small boys and they are both mine
And, of course, one is bigger than the other.
And it has been a hell of a hard time for the littler.
He was a baby, and he was plump
And there was much kissing and much dandling
And every woman whose children were grown
(Including his mother)
Looked at him
And grabbed.
Because he was so soft
Because he was so fat
Because he smiled so sweetly and had such a dimple
Just one dimple
In his cheek.

And women were nice.
And men were awful.
There was his brother—who tickled him
And sometimes pinched,
Who could ride a bike
And read a book
And go for walks alone with me.
Who could run the phonograph

The Bravest One

And turn on the lights
And open the refrigerator door
And cut his meat.

There was his father
Who smelled pretty bad
And talked very loud
And had bristles on his face
And kept wanting him not to be a baby any more.

Not to be a baby!
Not to be dandled, and hugged
And loved and kissed, by sweet-smelling, low-talking,
    smooth-faced women
Soft all over.

He stood, uneasily on his baby legs.
He cried, uncertainly, in his baby voice.
He clenched his star-fish hands, but never never had the
    will to hit.

Until the other day,
When he found out how much fun it can be to stand up
    tall.
To talk loud.

I told him to leave the table, not to be a baby, and he went.
At the door he stopped. "I only wanted a yes or no
    answer," he said.

"No," I shouted. He went on a little way.

He came back to the door.

"All right," he said. "Then the answer is no. I just wanted
yes or no."

Hallelujah, sing hey. There are two small boys and both are
mine.

And the second one is—I never thought the day would
come—

The bravest in the whole wide world.

Braver than the first—he never had to say it to his father,

Braver than me—I never dared to say it to mine.